Sisters
and
Prophets

Sisters and Prophets

Art and Story by

Mary Lou Sleevi

AVE MARIA PRESS NOTRE DAME, INDIANA 46556

About the author:

The twelve paintings in *Sisters and Prophets* continue Mary Lou Sleevi's probing for meaning. "I believe that art has a unique capability to 'make new,' and that there is little vision of church presented today that uses the power and beauty of that perspective." For many years she has been using her artistic gifts to explore what the scriptures have to say to women.

Sleevi, who did commercial art while in college (Avila and Marquette) and while raising five children, studied under the late Ralph de Burgos. When her husband Gene began studying for his degree in Pastoral Counseling, Mary Lou began to paint her women of scripture. Sixteen were presented in her first book *Women of The Word* (Ave Maria Press, 1990); two, "Lydia" and "Sarah," were published as fine art serigraphs in limited editions.

Her paintings have been exhibited widely throughout the Washington D.C. area—in galleries, churches, colleges and at retreats and conferences there and in other cities. They have been exhibited at an annual meeting of the National Conference of Catholic Bishops and in the rotunda of the United Methodist Building on Capitol Hill, and have been featured in the nationally syndicated television program "Real to Reel."

Scripture selections from *The New American Bible*, copyright © 1970 by the Confraternity of Christian Doctrine, Washington, DC, are all used with permission of the copyright owner. All rights reserved.

Excerpts from *The New Jerusalem Bible*, copyright © 1985 by Darton, Longman & Todd, Ltd. and Doubleday & Company, Inc. are reprinted by permission of the publisher.

International Standard Book Number: 0-87793-514-9

Library of Congress Catalog Card Number: 93-71540

Cover and text design by Katherine Robinson Coleman

Printed and bound in the United States of America.

Contents

Foreword _____ 7

Introduction _____ 9

The Dancing Flame _____ 17

Miriam _____ 21

Deborah _____ 31

Hannah _____ 41

The Earthen Vessel _____ 49

Anna _____ 55

A Woman of Faith and Blood _____ 63

Talitha _____ 71

The Seeker _____ 81

The Women of Easter _____ 91

A Mother and Four Daughters _____ 101

The Wisdom of Color _____ 113

Foreword

To my friend, God—
It's been a New Experience of the road with you.

Rain or shine, a real stretch.
We've covered miles alone each day—
though the brushes and pencils
of sisters and prophets
were never far behind. They waited.

Good to get outside. Keep a steady pace.
Without thinking,
I'd recognize you on familiar pathways,
without knowing you were there.
Sudden awareness (sometimes hindsight)
of a sisterly,
motherly,
womanly Presence.

Not much talking; just walking.
Invariably, I smile.

Little "presences," I call them.
Not like seeing your hand
in sunsets or crocuses.

7

Different. Direct. Attention-getting?
Like you want to be discovered!

I frame the moment,
carry it home.

An everyday walk,
a personal pilgrimage to Mother God . . .
and the experience
that it is She
who is making a pilgrimage
to me.

Passing by the other way.

Introduction

"Artists have trouble knowing when a work is done," Ralph deBurgos, my mentor, used to mumble as he strolled around art class. We may get that trait from God.

Time to open these hands and let go. Time to say to the sisters and prophets with whom I've spent countless hours in this room: Time to get out of here and mix with people!

We have shared more than space. We know each other well. I've loved looking at you to create portraits and stories, working two art forms together. Your eyes have stared back—a real creative knack! Being with you was no life in a cloister, and certainly not pious. I was never far from a mirror. It's been holy.

Spirituality and kinship deepened in Privileged Conversation we had together, some of it audible. A sister is a soul to whom I entrust my story. A prophet is a visionary who looks and talks back. We get through. Eventually, we're really honest with God and each other, and can say so in paint. (How paint discerns!) I end up feeling affirmed. Signing off. Smudged. And lighter!

Sisters and Prophets expands the collection of my paintings and reflections that began with *Women of the Word*. The earlier works continue to get around in a variety of places, among all kinds of people, women and men. An ecumenical presence, they have graced many walls.

The new grouping focuses attention on Light—developing, enveloping my colorful faces of women of scripture. Changing images. Not all are luminaries; some are obscure. I dug. I groped. I played. And as an artist I marveled at the interplay of light and dark they all presage.

I visualize and verbalize in a familiar vernacular of the arts. I connect back to our biblical sisters—who lived real and visionary faith—to be real in my own creative space. Justice issues and ministry (not confined to church) predominate, because these are *ever* largely women's issues—and gospel priorities. The stories are my reflections on the Journey of Light.

Where, oh where, is Sister Wisdom? In here and out there, she helps me understand that a woman who Believes will somehow seem, in this day and age, a little bit odd.

Time to express the hunger for Mother God. For me, it comes from the deep place where Jesus is. Paint reveals a truth of its own.

Art is . . . what we do to remember. And to re-member.

Painting with acrylics, I continue to use a very disciplined, contemporary art form, Hard Edge. I freely adapt, keeping its feel for the abstract and openness to interpretation. Implicit simplicity is its gifted teacher. As an artist, I choose Hard Edge because it can only be mastered till the next time, and it wins over my tendency to get complicated. To one who loves rounded lines, the flatness is always challenging.

Each painting was done before the reflection, and not as illustration. I develop story as an art form of its own. Hard Edge has a growing influence on my poetic writing style. How the words love to play! Within the context of biblical events, imagination runs free. Art and story work together, each retaining independence.

Story is personalized. In the language of art and Mystery, there is something unique and universal about what it expresses.

The reader/viewer may wonder how to use the book "best." As you like. Probably at intervals, long and short. I hope that, somehow, you will interrupt a pattern. Take a fresh approach with your head and heart in your own way. You may need to put old images on hold. You may want to spend some time just with pictures . . . or one picture . . . or with the stories. Flip back for close-ups. Linger wherever. You may or may not explore the scriptural references provided.

> Each story can say
> something new
> every time it is read.
> Each painting is always open
> to reveal something more.

Prophets, like artists, are here
to break the mold. Who is prophet?

Without confining by too much refining, biblical prophets
were persons known as inspired, as speaking for God, and
sometimes foretelling.

Given an earthbound Holy People, prophecy is truly a mix
of the divine with the human, a Gift of the Spirit to be eagerly
sought. Prophecy may involve a prelude, process, and point of
departure. Change.

I work and pray that seekers may find a touch of truth and
beauty here

> . . . in Miriam, who walks through walls in celebration;
> . . . in God as Mother or Spirit of Dance, revealing herself
>   in Time remarkably yours and mine;
> . . . in Anna, whose whole life said "Hello!" to God;
> . . . in the Seeker. Your own lost coin?
> . . . in Hannah-Here-*I*-Am . . .
> . . . in Deborah, who heard a new call and stood tall;
> . . . in the woman of Faith and Blood, where fringe had
>   such benefits;
> . . . in Four Daughters—and their mother—whose future is
>   unscripted.

May these and the others simply surprise you with light and color!

————————————

Only one person on earth knows the whole story (well, most of it) on the messy trail of paint here—Gene, my husband. To say thank you is redundant. Your touch—or smudge (to be continued)—is on each page. As happens on a long journey together. Keep your coat on.

Three of our friends who impacted both *Women of the Word* and *Sisters and Prophets* moved to heaven as this book was being completed. Thanks . . .

Sister Pat O'Haire, for sharing with such conviction your first and last Verse: "You will know the truth and the truth will set you free." What a seeker!

Lucile Doyle, who died without our goodbyes at age ninety-one. My painting "The Women of Easter" was complete the day you died—except for the face of Mary of Magdala. I did it that night.

And Bill Ferrando, Caterer to God. What a natural at *the* banquet table. In the week of your dying, I wrote Talitha's story. Your trademark was that classy, arty beret—your flair for living.

————————————

Artists have trouble knowing when work is done. Time to open these hands and let go. Time to say to you persons and prophets: read on, stare back! Where you find something of beauty—yourself—here, linger.

Mary Lou Sleevi
Reston, Virginia

God, shod in fire, touches down on the dance floor of Earth.

The Dancing Flame

(Adapted from Luke 12:49; Hebrews 12:29)

From the beginning,
Light
plays
in the dark.

Sparks fly.
Morning stars.
The Spirit choreographs
a Leap.

God, shod in Fire,
touches down
on the dance floor
of Earth . . .

. . . loving to do
the old soft-shoe—
a tap dance without taps.

Keeping time to the pounding of each human heart—
upbeat, downbeat,
offbeat.

She is imaging
the Dancer
in a whole new way.

Hold her hand.
There is light!

Miriam dances down the great long Aisle. The walk itself is Celebration.

Miriam

(Exodus 2:1-10; 15:20-21; Numbers 12; 20:1; Micah 6:4)

Passage
comes at a time when a prophet
taught a world to dance.

Miriam, sister of Moses and Aaron,
reared, as it were, to a limited role,
wisely used walls
exceedingly well.

She made the most of God-given Opportunity—
not just squeezing by.

In childhood, she had asked a Question
at the Right Time.
It worked.
That in itself makes her
a Major Prophet for our day.
Shall we present
the Fun One as well?

She dances down the great long Aisle.
The walk itself is Celebration.

21

Water plays
like rain in her face.
Feels good. Let it come!
Rain is my sister—
like wind in the air.
Be in my hair!
Brush.

God-in-The-Cloud
rolled a Red Carpet
down the floor
of a parted sea.

Art enters in
between night and morning.
A seascape of Water Walls
letting people go.

It may be the first Interpretation
bubbling through the deep
to be portrayed by a woman,
leading women.

Apparently they crossed
with particular flourish.
The prophet up-front, named as such,
takes up her tambourine.
Song of the spirit—a very free spirit—
reaches staccato pitch.

Dancing through walls
to their left and right,
all the women follow.
Give them room; let them go!
Exulting, exclaiming,
they pre-date and precede us,
this freedom train.
As mover and shaker of Liberation,
Moses, move over.

Dancers got their feet wet
saluted by seas
with Frolicking Foam.
It was not all play.
There's muscle behind those pointed toes
and rounded arches!
More than gesture in waving arms!

Not so much bending.
Time to stretch backs!
Less pirouetting—
that graceful rotation,
that Spinning Around.

Miriam leads the procession
in the way God's people
Go. On Purpose!

23

As *we* emerge
over the hill,
she grows in the role
of Prophet of Dance.
She was made for the Part.

Notice. One cannot but notice.
She has no fear of falling in.
We put the face and the Feat
on those who come after.

She's so vividly *present*!
Visibility
in a Red Dress.
Though it be fraught
with Larger meaning,
the original design
is to be
festive.

To us
Miriam bequeaths her Dancing Dress.
In the meantime,
enjoy a moment.

Water relates fundamentally
to the ups and downs
that people the salvation story.

When Jesus walked *on* water,
that was *another* dance.
And quite a dance-*floor*! Ask Peter.

It's a footnote to remember
when the world seems
flat.

———————————

We first meet Miriam
securing the future
of her brother and their people.

There were so many Hebrews
in the Land of Oppression
that Pharaoh ordered the drowning
of all their infant males.
But the Robust People were resourceful.

When baby Moses could no longer be hidden,
he was placed in a papyrus basket
"among the reeds at the River's edge.
His sister took up position some distance away
to see what would happen to him."

Pharaoh's daughter came to bathe in the river,
shadowed by maids patrolling its Border.
When the basket was discovered
and the child well-received,
the prophet-in-waiting ambled out.

Miriam didn't tiptoe;
she asked the pertinent Question.
"Shall I go and find you a nurse among the
Hebrew women to nurse the child for you?"

"Yes, do!" she was answered.
So "the girl went and called
the child's own mother."

The boy was named Moses,
for, said Pharaoh's daughter,
"I drew him out of the water."

———————————————

Through the years, Miriam re-appears
for song and dance,
dissent and punishment.
It is also noted that she died and was buried.
Most of Exodus and beyond
ignores her.

Let her not, in the dark of wilderness,
become less the Celebrating Prophet
accomplished and admired.
She knew how to sing
and also to speak.

She could dance or stand firm,
indomitably
(while Moses, it is said,
was "the meekest man on the face of the earth").
Who was threatened
by her influence?
Did she make waves?

She has a touch of the Tragic Figure,
struck "white as snow"
by skin disease, probably of short duration.
Miriam was banished from camp for seven days
of Cleansing.
She had found fault with Moses.

Had not Aaron and the others?
Miriam was singled out—so colorfully!

    Why? God knows.
    And good people
    ask good questions
    of one another.

Some things don't have a clear connection.
But that's a different story.

Her smile remains wistful.
Miriam would not have donned Sackcloth.

27

The prophet Micah wrote,
"For I brought you up from Egypt,
I ransomed you from the place of slave labor
and sent
Moses, Aaron, and Miriam to lead you."

———————————

A sister asked a Question
at the Right Time and Place.

New ones roll in and around us
bubbling up from baptism.
They are more than Froth.

See the Sea!
May crashing waves
remind us of Miriam.
Feel the splashing!
It's just Miriam's Mist.

On Deborah's head is the royal purple of leadership, on her shoulders
rests the blue Mantle of wisdom and peace.

Deborah

(Judges 4:1-14; 5)

The only woman ever to be
Judge of Israel
    —in the days before Monarchy
    when the land was ruled by judges—
steps away from the Court
where she Sat
at the Palm Tree on the Mountain.

The Verdict is in.
Arise, arise, Mother of Israel!
Deborah,
at once retrospective
and introspective,
considers perspectives and prospects.

Standing,
the prophet who inspired the Song of Deborah
contends with the Command of God
that she delivered. It will be Enacted.
Her own word is given
at the risk of her life.

"I to the Lord will sing my song,
my hymn to . . . the God of Israel."

In a lonely, lovely Interlude,
her fingers ping a string of a lyre.
The wind picks up, its fragrance balmy.

The sun, symbol of Justice in the ancient East,
rises with her,
and colors the skies—a little.

 Deborah, prophet and wife,
 "was judging Israel at the time.
 She used to sit under Deborah's Palm . . .
 in the highlands of Ephraim,
 and the Israelites would come to her
 for justice."

Up the hillside to her tree,
trodding with troubles large and small,
feet beat a path each day.

God and people trusted her
as one of their own.
She had summoned Barak to the mount
to give him God's Instructions:
Go. March.

The warrior was to lead a great army
to win a decisive victory
for the freedom of the Israelites.

But Barak had answered the judge:
"'If you come with me, I will go;
if you do not come with me,
I will not go.'"
For he would not know
how to choose the day
when God would grant him success.

"'I will certainly go with you,'" she replied,
immediately reinforcing the word.
(She also told him that Sisera, the enemy general,
would fall at the hands of a woman.)
Deborah marched with Barak;
an army of ten thousand men were behind them.
"Up!" she discerned on the Day of Deliverance
that happened as she had said.

The Prophet and Judge
has a good inner ear.
She hears from both sides,
weighs and balances head and heart.
With uncommon sense and its sister, wisdom,
she draws on her own Intelligence report.
She will judge rightly.

She may have been elevated to leadership
more by the ability to make hard decisions
with knowledge and foresight
than to counsel pastorally
in the shade of the palm tree.

Perhaps her Stature—
    her Genius, her Legacy—
combines both.

Distinctively, instinctively,
the woman invests *herself*.
It seems fitting to appropriate the Kithara,
an ancient lyre,
for the hands of Deborah,
commemorating her fine Sense of Touch.

To the leader of Israel,
the liberation of an oppressed people
is a recurrent Theme-Song,
known by heart
and always played by ear.

    Deborah's Song,
    one of the oldest surviving fragments
    of Hebrew Poetry,
    connects poignantly
    with the ongoing Theme of salvation history:
    God's presence with People.

"The villages in Israel were no more,
they were no more,
until you arose, O Deborah!
until you arose, Mother of Israel!"

Less than idyllic, mountaintop living
takes her head out of the clouds.
One sees there.
Sometimes too much.
Of conflict, inside and out.

Looking up or down
or all around
wakes up, makes up, shakes up
Vision. Point of view.
The air up there
is purifying!

In Deborah's quiet times,
the mountain had taught her
the essence of Quiescence.
The Storm will follow.

Only the name of her husband, Lappidoth,
is told in the story.
The advocate of Peace and Justice
is no portrait of a wife
in soft, shaded Pastels.

35

On her head is the royal purple
of leadership,
born of a passion for people
who also are God's.

As nature bestows a windy anointing,
the sun "fractures the image"
of purple oppression
which is to be broken
as the prophet has spoken.

On Deborah's shoulders
rests the blue Mantle of wisdom and peace
(never without its throwback to purple),
which will reign with her for forty years.

Touching her mountaintop
with an instrument of music,
the purple of anguish locates
the fertile green of hope.

God's personal instrument is Deborah.
The distant high lands of promise
are rolling right through her;
their summits also an image
fractured by sunlight.

Justice and peace merge
in tranquil violets and cerulean blues—
hues that are the future of her people,
at least in Deborah's Day.

The climactic episode
in the Epic of Deborah and her Era of Peace
is the death of the cruel Sisera
from a drink and a peg
in the hands of the jabbing Jael.

But the Liberation Song, however fragmented
—written *about* Deborah, not *by* her—
is the love song of a grateful people.

As she leads celebration,
its lyrics begin:
"They sang a song that day,
Deborah and Barak!"

Who stands as sister
to Deborah today?

One wise enough
to hope, dream, show her colors.

A believer
—because she is
the woman she is—
does these things
and sings.

"Let those who love you
be like the sun," the anthem ends . . .
emerging in all its strength!
For love of justice,
the kiss of peace is given.

And Deborah lived to see it.

At last was Hannah-Here-I-Am terribly, unbearably, herself.

Hannah

(1 Samuel 1; 2:1-10, 18-21; 3:1-10)

A Spark came down from The Lamp in The Shrine
and caught a Great Tear,
dropping into the cup
of an open hand.

Her eyes know,
and her fingers—
loosening up on the empty tiny tunic.
This is *Hannah*-Here-I-Am,
whose lips may have moved to a first Magnificat
there at the Shrine of Shiloh.

Long before Samuel said,
"Here I am,"
three times one night in this very place,
his Mother Prophet was there,
time after time, year after year,
faithfully,
fruitlessly.

And Here came Hannah back again,
wondering why.

Here . . .
in a space to embrace that darkness where light is;
to risk that Peculiar Kind of Sight
given only by the Heavens at night.
In her hallowed hour, she was all hollow;
Hannah was caving in.

The Lamp was dim in the Sacred Shrine.
It mused
in murky, misty grays,
brushing them lightly, slightly, with purple.
It perused
the face of Hannah,
exceptionally done, this Feastday,
in watercolors.

To the family, back at Shiloh,
gathered nearby for the sacred meal,
this course of Pilgrimage
was all too familiar.
Husband Elkanah
was again beside himself.
His other wife, less-loved
but happily so fruitful,
was about her Great Love of harassing Hannah.
Peninnah would make a whole pilgrimage of it,
with Her-Glory-The-Children in tow.

And Elkanah would ask—tenderly, tensively, apprehensively:
    "Hannah, why weep?
    Why refuse to eat and drink?
    Why be unhappy?
    Am I not enough for you?"

She may well have favored him there, this time,
with a forthright:
    "Frankly, no."
Hannah had had it.

Void of Virtue-By-The-Womb,
she swept away from the meal at the shrine,
and leapt, crept, and cried
toward Light, directly,

    "Lord, remember me. *Remember* me?
    Give me a son,
    and I will give him back to you
    for as long as he lives."

Bittersweetly,
a torrent of words
—classically deferential—
formed in her "mother" tongue.
Hannah prayed from a lonely cave.

She stayed a long time under The Lamp,
those wonderless eyes wondrously weeping.
Something holy inside
shied,
virtually died for expression.

And something wonderful happened in the dark
that nobody saw or heard.
The breakthrough, the person called to be,
was not a child
but an adult woman,
born in her night
with parent God.

At last was Hannah-Here-*I*-Am,
terribly,
unbearably
herself.

"Aha!" God cried out,
disclosing her Presence.
"I-Am-Right-Here-With-You."

The brooding creative Spirit,
who seldom appears in standardized form,
does show Originality somehow or other
Splendidly.

Hannah's words came to fall
in a squall of silence.
Eli, the high priest, on duty at the door,
surprised, mesmerized,
by the quietly moving mouth (he was used to loud pray-ers)
thought she was drunk (though not by the Spirit).

"How much longer are you going to stay drunk?
Get rid of your wine!"
. . . broke from the man who knew all the norms
of feastday celebrations.

But Hannah came through truly,
and Eli warmed to whisper:
"Go in peace . . . and God grant you . . . whatever."

Then a Spark came down
from The Lamp in The Shrine,
and caught a Great Tear,
dropping into the cup
of an open hand.

The Tear caught Fire.
Her eyes, softly, suddenly, show
they Know.
Fingers loosen up on the tiny tear-touched tunic.

A White Tunic, sign of consecration.
Like an empty canvas
is Hannah's work of art.

In her handwork—such a small thing!—
are emptiness and holding fast,
prerequisites
to most exquisite art.

Hannah, perused,
is the hurt place where heart is,
where art is.
Truth come to Beauty
of person and prayer.

Surely an ultimate Risk of Light
is to hold onto and upmost
what is closest and utmost,
then open the hand and let go.

So that the artist and the
artwork can move beyond.

Hannah's peace and her appetite
returned that night at Shiloh.
The whole family left for home
in the dim light of morning.

Hannah and Elkanah
conceived a son, of course,
and in early childhood
Samuel-Here-I-Am
entered service with Eli at Shiloh.
Eli never got over her Initiative—
or Hannah.
She was Epoch-Making.

Hannah grew.
She knew how to make decisions.
Her prayer was not stuck or sticky.
Eli observed
she was swallowing far less salt.

A Magnificat of Exultation became Hannah's Song.
She and her husband had other children.
(Eli always blessed them
as they were turning home.)

Time after time,
they'd come back
to Shiloh and Samuel.
The Prophet brought a tunic
made in larger size.

This was *Hannah*-Here-I-Am.
Here I am. Here I *am*. Here *I* am . . . hear, dear God!

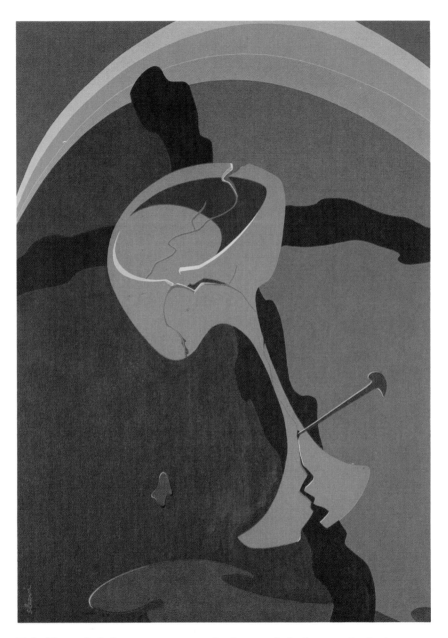

Behold, nailed there on a cross, the battered chalice is the body of Emmanuel.

The Earthen Vessel

(Adapted from 2 Corinthians 4:6-15; Galatians 3:28)

Breaking of skies
unifies
the Friday and Sunday
that are Eucharist-making.
Darkness and light
form a backdrop of Easter.

People, just people,
come together at a Rainbow Bend.
Behold,
nailed there on a cross,
the battered chalice
is
the body of Emmanuel.

God-With-Us.
The wood that bears him
is a rain forest
of hurt
and of healing.

Shattered,
The Earthen Vessel
spills out empty on earth.

Empty is full.
We too are made
a cup of blessing . . .
together re-forming a body of Christ
co-creative and re-creative.

Earthbound Jesus
expands our circumference,
sometimes explosively.
We are done in.

Just Peace remains.

We breathe deeply.

Faith ever fragile
is the way to go
free.

Witness . . .
It becomes more crucial
to stand for
than kneel to.

And to confront the Perfect Stranger
inside the whole broken cup,
base to brim.

"Emmanuel, is it *you?*"
This is . . .
where we come from,
the cutting edge,
the Measure where church is—
or is not.

It strikes us
like the first time,
all over again.

Edges are cutting
for people who live there.
Cracks desecrate and disfigure
those who fall through
(like soil that cracks
and writes hunger on bodies).

In Christ, without hedges,
one is all
who thirst for uprightness;
they shall be filled.

There are no second-class people,
no third world or first,
no woman or man.

One body is raised.

Sisters and prophets of an Easter people
tell the others.
Again and again.

Wonderfully,
with all our rough edges,
we come together
in The Earthen Vessel . . .
raised to be parts
of a Cup of Blessing.

Be. Hold.

We do this
to remember.

Anna comes to Her Moment laughing. Those eyes have twinkled
as she wrinkled.

Anna

(Luke 2:22-38; Matthew 5:8)

Her laugh is simply happy.

The prescribed pair of turtledoves,
averse to captivity,
refrain for the moment
from their soft, plaintive moans.

From their perch
they lurch forward
to take in The Occasion.

Exuberantly,
Anna recognizes a child
at his Presentation in the temple.
She talks of him
in no uncertain terms!
Her particular words are shrouded,
but Delight registers profoundly
under the veil of widow-black.

A lifetime of focus
is all in her eyes.
Thanks be to God!

55

The old woman is truly Beautiful
and beautifully True.

Her passage of scripture,
that follows the heralded Word of Simeon,
reads:

"There was also a certain prophetess,
Anna by name,
daughter of Phanuel of the tribe of Asher.
She had seen many days,
having lived seven years with her husband . . .
and then as a widow until she was eighty-four.
She was constantly in the temple,
worshipping day and night
in fasting and prayer.

"Coming on the scene at this moment,
she gave thanks to God
and talked about the child
to all who looked forward
to the deliverance of Jerusalem."

Anna comes to Her Moment laughing,
her face the free expression
of all that's inside.

Her life of late
seems to have staged
an ongoing soliloquy.
That heavenly smile authenticates Anna.

She is the Recognized Prophet
who came and confirmed
the word of a brother who said,
"'My eyes have witnessed your saving deed
displayed for all the peoples to see . . .'"

As phophets do,
Anna ensured that the message
would get beyond temple precincts.

She probably heard Simeon speak,
and may have embellished
his Inspiration
by extending her hugs to the Chosen parents.
Very tenderly.

Anna had seen it all.
Grown-ups talk anxiously
about fulfilling the dreams of children.
Anna's Jesus-Moment
is an elder's consummate Belief
in a dream come true.

She speaks truth beautifully,
naturally.
The gift of prophecy is backed
by her life/prayer of eighty-four years.

Stretch marks
from solitude and solicitude and solidarity
show in The Wrinkling,
giving her face its certain Lift.

Anna of the free Spirit
is no solemn ascetic.
She talks *to* the baby,
as well as about him.
She shoulders him closely,
absorbing his softness,
his heartbeat,
his breathing—
experiencing a Benediction of Years
between them.
This is Manifestation embodied.

Solace.
The prophet knows
she has looked at him.

Years later,
words of Jesus would Beatify her vision:
"Blest are the single-hearted
for they shall see God."

Those eyes have twinkled
as she wrinkled.

"Constantly in the temple,"
the temple of her heart,
she became familiar
with every inch of her living space
—including its limitations—
and the Beneficence of Sister Wisdom
dwelling therein.
Anna liked the view from her window.
And a comfortable chair.

In "worshipping day and night,"
she had spent her Vitality
on an extravagance of prayer,
and discovered she was strong.

Life with Wisdom was a trilogy
of faith, hope, and love.
In Anna's everyday Essence,
love of God and faith in a people—
and
faith in God and love of a people—

59

were insatiable and inseparable.
And her fasting produced
a Gluttony of hope.

The disciplined disciple,
never withdrawn,
stayed in touch with the world
and kept finding God.

Once
upon his time,
she welcomed The Promised One.

"She talked about the child . . ."
And talk Anna did.
She is more than prophet:
she is a grandmother!

Because it is the Christ-child she hugs,
Anna, as prophet,
is particularly aware
of the vulnerability of less-awaited children
and parents,
who also have dreams.

———————————————

Anna.
Dimming eyes,
still forward-looking,
crinkle with joy.
Anna is Anticipation.

She is an Image
of constancy and change . . .
the progression of peace and purpose
at any stage of life.

Hers is the Holy City.

Solitude
as Anna lived it
lessens fear of the death-moment.
With God, one never stops saying
"Hello!"

The hand of one who is not allowed to touch much gets through to him.

A Woman of Faith and Blood

(Mark 5:25-34; Matthew 9:20-22; Luke 8:43-48)

Even the Homespun
looked worn to a frazzle.

The crowd almost crushed him
on the way to the House of Jairus.
Nerves frayed.
James and John, among the disciples,
barely kept their composure
in that enclosure
of so many Cloaks.

Peter, of course, was hardly unflappable.
When Jesus asked, "'Who touched me?'"
Peter flared. He glared.
"'You can see how this crowd hems you in!'"
Jesus insisted,
"'Someone touched me:
I know that power has gone forth from me.'"

63

Someone on that Pilgrimage,
This Woman,
pressed and pushed by all that is flapping
around and about her,
takes a deep breath
and stretches herself.
The hand of one who is
not allowed to touch
much
(because of blood flow)
gets through to him.

"'If I just touch his clothing,'"
she thought perspicaciously,
"'I shall get well.'"

Audaciously, efficaciously
reaching out to the hem of Jesus' mantle,
she grabs its tassel
of violet thread,
the ancient sign of a Consecrated People.

(Tassels in shades of Purple,
commonly fastened on four corners of a mantle,
expressed a Meaning of Heritage
among People who knew first-hand
all the colors and fringes
and scratchiness
of everyday religious wear.

Such are the "hems" of scripture,
familiar in stories of healing.)

Hemmed in, the woman holds on.
Maybe not tight or fast.
For the moment, at least,
it is all she can do to simply hold on.

Instantly, her bleeding—
a worsening hemorrhage of twelve years' duration
whose treatment had dried up only her savings—
stopped.

In its place, "the feeling that she was cured . . .
ran through her whole body."

"Who touched me?"
Wheeling about (so it is written),
Jesus persisted in looking around.

Her smile hardly hides.
She lays a hand on a cloak
—any old cloak—
that is blocking her way.

It is a Magnificent Move.

Her dark veil,
the color of mourning
and prophets,
falls back.

Her drabness of dress
loses some of its gray.

    Nonetheless,
    paint tells her-story
    in her hollows and hair.
    Clearly, this is a face
    of faith with no frills.

    Blood disease
    had placed her doubly in jeopardy
    because she is woman.

Beginning to tremble as she realized what happened,
the pre-emptive prophet came up front
and told the Truth in Her Eyes
to him and the whole assembly.

"'Daughter,'" Jesus said directly,
"'It is your faith that has cured you.
Now go in peace.'"

Jesus had a habit
of turning things around.
Significantly,
in deference to woman,
this healing may be an Adaptation
of the messianic truism:
No life is given
without the issue of blood.

Wisdom Turns on the Light.
Sometimes the signal
is straight ahead.

Go. Faith keeps its feet on the ground
and thrives in mid-air,
Occasionally.
Faith is so incarnate
it Breathes.

Healing Power, so shocked by Faith,
absorbs it.

Jesus was profoundly aware
of Healing Energy
between him and someone—
in particular;

and fully confident then and there
that God was sending him further,
to bother,
to command, "Talitha, kum!"

Jesus and
this sick-and-tired Woman
walked, stumbling, into their Given Moment,
together in the tag-along life
of all sorts of fringe people,
including believers.

Fringe has its benefits.

Each in the company
with the heart of a pilgrim (under wraps, perhaps),
found a fork in the road
a good place to stretch.

Though it gets sidetracked,
Faith is always on the way.
Usually somewhere else.
Or so it would seem.

Faith is a Journey of Jumps,
    bumps,
    slumps,
    grumps,
    and grins.

Go? Where?
A couple of prophets
out there
received a Word of Knowledge
on the road to the House of Jairus.

Such is a way
toward Healing and Peace.
It started from scratch.

So-o-o
Where?
Oh, the pressures!
Some days, in all the flapping and the dangling,
it is all one can do
to hold on,
barely,
simply to you,
Jesus.

The Artist's Smock is a Homespun Cloak.

Loosen up
and don't let go
is the word from this woman's hand.

On the threshold of womanhood, Talitha is expressly empowered to live growing up.

Talitha

(Mark 5:21-43; Matthew 9:18-26; Luke 8:40-56)

The life she had known
had faded away,
but her eyesight engages
a whole New Day.

In a dark, curtained room,
a trail winds home
to death's Disruption.
On the face of a child
is faith's Eruption,
perhaps by virtue
of an Interruption.

As at the Raising of Lazarus,
Jesus used late arrival
to break a favorite word of Abundant Life:
Be not afraid!

Milestones and pebbles—and undergrowth—
may require anyone anytime
to take a Leap
or just go on Walking.

But it is the byway of Interruption
that keeps faith Fluid.

Almost simultaneously,
Jesus decided on all three Courses
on the road this day.
The third may take priority,
especially this day.

"'Who touched me?'" he had asked.
Such a commotion!
The clutch at his cloak
got lost in the shove
of the shuffling crowd around him.
But Power reacted to Pain abruptly.
And a woman, scared, stiffened
for a second.

He knew and she knew
the Trauma and the Drama.
Her healing propelled Jesus
to a twelve-year-old's side,
even unto death.

"Talitha, kum!"
The original Aramaic words
have survived intact
in most English translations of the New Testament.

They are like creed.
We also like to *say* them!

Quotation remarks, acquired over time,
often soften edges.

Let us appropriate the quote
directly,
Entitling a person
to a First Name
with character all its own.

"Talitha."
It's lovely. It lilts. It lingers on the tongue.
And is inspired by his.

Taking her hand tightly.
bending only slightly
without speaking down,
Jesus *commanded*, make no mistake:
"Get up, little girl!"
Bother me.

On the threshold of womanhood.
Talitha is expressly empowered
to live
growing up.

She is named to be Potential,
to change, to develop.
It is Speech with Fecundity—
Persuasive Eloquence
of the highest order.

She will See.
She is focused. She is challenged.

Jesus' word is made flesh
in the heart of Talitha.
Hands are used as the Transfer Point.
What a surge!
Life in its fullness
is indubitably Transforming.

    Heroines—like childhood saints—
    are always made larger than life.
    Talitha, after all,
    was once just a girl
    or someone's kid sister.

    Today she will be "person,"
    not a little saint.
    It may be holy
    to be all she can be.

Talitha will take wing
from those who taught her to walk
over undergrowth.
Father Jairus, a synagogue official,
who kept his stride
all the way to Jesus
and back again,
never just "went along" for the ride.

"'My little daughter is critically ill,'" he had said.
"'Please come and lay your hands on her
so that she may get well and live.'"
He had a dream
for this child
that was mirrored in the eyes of another Dreamer.

They walked together.
In the crowd that followed
was the woman who touched off a hassle
by touching a tassel.

Interception and Intercession
are not worlds apart.

When word came, "'Your daughter is dead.
Why bother the Teacher further?'"
Jesus interrupted all talk of stopping.
"'Fear is useless.
What is needed is trust.'"

75

His words found Jairus,
who might have been a bit dubious about then.
But Jairus *acted*
as if he believed.
An unpretentious Act of Determination.
To be continued.

When they arrived at the house full of Mourners,
faith was met with its real opposition
whose group name is Fear.
"She's *dead*, not asleep!"
was laughed in derision.

Fear looks dimly
at Light beyond sight.
Fear was cast out.

The weepers and wailers
with their non-stop lamenting
were kept in the cold.

In its many disguises,
fear freezes people
more than lack of faith.

But the parents of Talitha
—with Jesus, Peter, James, and John—
entered a cubicle
and created a Sanctuary.

Without knowing or second-guessing
where new Life would lead,
the father and mother,
rooted in tradition,
paved the way, opened the door, and went in
—probably ahead of Jesus—
certainly before the apostles.

To be open to God,
they got up from their own cradling pillows
and security blankets.
Yes . . . life would be different,
they trusted.

Hum-m-m-m. Humph-h-h?
"The family's astonishment knew no bounds."
Awe eyes them.

Hold on to Talitha securely,
sending her forth.
She gives cause
to pause in our weeping.
(The woman before her
did more than stop bleeding.)

Her name carries indelibly
to a new generation of church,
and to the old,
the in-between,
and anyone who has felt
that life is over—
at least in church.

Some find it comatose or already dead.

Tomorrow will be shaped
by today's "little girls."
Called to mature,
Talitha must step forward
to keep church Alive.

> Once our eyes have been opened,
> a prophetic sense knows
> there is more going on
> than the eye can see.

> Have you ever discerned
> by its perceptible light
> a face that has looked on Jesus?

> It makes the heart flutter
> to recognize him
> or her
> in the eyes of another.

Faith sees—
with contact lenses
precision-made in heaven.

Gray.
More goes into its subtleties
beneath the surface.
Far more than neither/nor.

Sometimes
an Interruption of Light
flickers—like a signal.

Life will never be the same.

———————————————

"Give her something to eat,"
Jesus, Bread of Life,
directed.

It was undoubtedly the mystified mother,
already poised,
who ran all the way to the oven.

The undervalued Coin she seeks may be to her a pearl of great price.

The Seeker

(Luke 15:8-10)

Around the house
there is always This Broom
in a room.
Usually women push it . . .
diligently.

This Woman puts fine focus
on a spot on the floor . . .
directing lamplight,
enlarging its sphere.
She is credited with an Eye for Detail.

Women identify the worker
in particularly personal terms,
"She's like a sister to me."
And oh, those miscellanies
—like little plastic pieces—
under The Broom!

In a world that's a zone of disordered time,
a litany of "Just a Minute!"
sets the standard for a day.

So much that is longed for
can't be reached in
just a minute.

The undervalued Coin she seeks
may be to her
a pearl of great price.

She can name it
by herself.
She may name it
herself.

With eyes trained on the job,
her Broom stalks the floor
she walks every day.

In a corner, so to speak,
between the memorable and memorized
parables of Jesus
about a lost sheep and a prodigal son,
is a Metaphor for God
less impressed on Mother Church.

    "'What woman,
    if she has ten silver pieces
    and loses one,
    does not light a lamp

and sweep the house
in a diligent search
until she has retrieved what she lost?

"'And when she finds it,
she calls in her friends and neighbors
to say,
'Rejoice with me!
I have found the silver piece
I lost!'

"'I tell you,
there will be the same kind of joy
before the angels of God
over one repentant sinner.'"

The scriptural Image reflects on
a common ground of Experience.
"What woman does not . . ." do these things?
asks the opening verse.

For anyone,
Sweeping with God
is a walk and a work
—more likely a Work-Out and very healthy;
the Broom an outward sign
that God knows where to get pushy.

83

Hands on.
Hers is a Blueprint
of Owning and Acting:
of Responsibility for "Change":

>She has,
>she loses,
>she lights,
>she sweeps,
>she finds,
>she calls,
>she leads celebration.

"Everywoman" of church
is searching sacred ground.
Hunger for God
is Woman's great corporate Charism,
and a basic Gift of the Spirit
to church in the world.

Given many forms,
it's been taken for granted;
and is less than acknowledged
as core
anymore.

But it can't be dismissed.
It will insist; it will persist;
and it will prevail.

It works its way out,
so we sweep while we weep.
Diligent in Initiative,
we do not beat the air
in a hold of despair.
Well, sometimes . . . in the dark.

Reality Spirituality
opens a way.

Eyes on.
"What woman does not . . ."
re-evaluate—time, work, and money?
Her own.

We've been told so often
such things don't count much
that we bought the idea
right here in church.
We are unlearning.

Plainly, what women do more of
is time-consuming, energy-eating
and marked-down in market value.

As church that we are in the world,
we push toward just employment—
as in Living Wage.

We redefine ceilings and glass,
and levels of entry
and ethics.

The ethos of minority
is rejected by us prophets
because we are Come of Age.
Minority status
(used relatively,
meaning lesser and subordinate)
is not gone for good.

The status Quo is disallowed.
Much tripping on Guilt is disavowed.
The Broom is an outward sign
of an inner room.

We are stepping out and sorting through.
The Coin swept under the rug so long
has much to do with Self-Appraisal.
We *take* our time: we own it.
This changes Reality
and changes Spirituality.

Woman's search for identity
closely relates to Hunger for God.
She struggles
to be a real person in her world.

She has to be.

Beyond the miscellanies
(under a broom that is sometimes plastic)
what's real about me, God?
What's real about you?

    That's the Risk of the Broom
    and the Fear of the Dark.

    God does not light the wick;
    I do.
    Good God, why *me*?

    Because you will do these things,
    speaks from the heart.

    You reach for the stars
    with your eyes on Good Earth.

In all corners of the globe,
minority status
devalues
enormous numbers of people.
It marks off
places, races, faces
to deprivation
larger than life.
One
doesn't count much.

Disproportionately high numbers of women
never have coins to lose. Not a one.
To be hungry
is not understood
in its Larger Meaning.

Their floor is the ground,
literally bed and board.
They have learned where they come from
the hard way:
most have no place to go.
There's no oil
and no lamp.
And yet they believe in God.

An undervalued Coin,
A Pearl of great price,
is brought to the fore.

The Architect
who designed All Room
turns up the light.

Women gather around The Rock to tell their stories and to believe one another.

The Women of Easter

(Mark 14: 8; 15:40; 16:1-11; John 11:1-44; 12:1-8; 20:1-18;
Luke 8:1-3; Matthew 20:20-23)

Later in the morning
on the first day of the week,
when it is no longer dark,
women gather around The Rock
to tell their stories
and to believe one another.

"Here!" says Mary of Magdala.
"He was standing right here."
"'Woman . . . why are you weeping?'" he asked.
"'Who is it you are looking for?'"
   And then he said,
   "'Mary!'"
"Right here," she says. Transfixed.

With a supportive hug
someone else tries to see.
Crocuses that cluster
attend at her feet.

91

This is a way it might have been
in a circle of friends that Sunday . . .
There was a focused group
who had kept the three-day Watch
that became for them
a total Experience
of Easter.

They had traveled in his company.
Each had decided
earlier in the ministry of Jesus
to follow him.
Clear identities are often uncertain.

Some had been healed,
cured of evil spirits and maladies.
Some had assisted the daily Work
out of their means.
All
change.

There was a larger assortment of friends
who moved to him.
Verse-lines on women of Holy Week
are inclusive of many "others,"
around particular persons.

A common sense is Compassion.
Women disciples
made the first Way of the Cross.

From close-up and afar,
they saw Calvary.
Women observed the tomb that was hewn,
and how Jesus was buried.
They Observed the Sabbath.

The First Few to arrive
on the site of Easter
were told to tell the brothers
and others.

    Who would want to come back
    later in the morning?
    From the gospel stories,
    who was likely last to leave . . . ?

    Why, women of course.

Certainly Salome
    and "the other Mary"
along with Mary of Magdala.

The three
had stood at the cross
and had stooped in the tomb
    in the dark before dawn,

intending to anoint the body
they had seen laid to rest.

    Salome, wife of Zebedee,
    was mother of James and John,
    those "sons of thunder"
    notably present in gospel scenes
    in most transforming moments.

    Mary of Clopas, called the "other Mary,"
    was parent of James and Joset,
    probably younger disciples.
    Once the grave had been sealed,
    Joseph and Nicodemus went away.
    Two Marys remained there,
        watching and waiting
        in front of the tomb.

A certain Joanna, mentioned as a traveler,
is also closely identified
with the Easter companions.

    The wife of Herod's steward Chuza,
    she may have left her husband behind
    as well as the lifestyle of The Court.

Susanna might have come, a relative unknown,
another sister-traveler in the company of Jesus.
She, too, had been healed.

On this Morning of all mornings,
why not include the sisters he loved so much?
Mary and Martha live close by,
where he stopped of late
on the way to Jerusalem.

And the memorable woman/prophet
who had anointed him Last Week . . .

And probably,
others.
It seems there was always another Mary.
Did someone bring his mother
for a Moment?

———————————————————

What did they do?
How do they cope, fearful and trembling,
in that inner, outer circle?

Probably together.
Women who fled from the tomb
would never have gone fishing.
Nor to Emmaus.

They ran and reported
and then they Returned.
Presently they stayed There,
at least for a while.

95

The Feel of Resurrection
is in fingers, feet, and eyes.
The Sound of Resurrection
tells in one another's stories.

They take their time now;
let it happen to them.
They go back in the tomb,
touching, retouching, walls and wrappings.

    If Martha is absent
    she's been fetching bread
    for forgotten appetites.
    What a morning for late Breakfast!
    What a time to break Fast
    on that Rock for a table!

They talk.
Salome was not shy about speaking up
at profound moments.
(How she had tried to promote her sons
on the road to Jerusalem!)
She reviews the conversation with Jesus
and is not embarrassed.
Not a word is forgotten.

Magdalene, still stunned by "Do not cling to me . . . !"
and shunned by brothers' Disbelief,
clutches a rock
because there's no place to go.

Does she reflect on Martha's recent words
at the grave of brother Lazarus,
"Lord, if you had been here . . ."
"Even now I am sure . . ."
"I have come to believe . . ."

Mary of Bethany, with her poet's memory,
relives every word he said one day
when she listened at his feet.

The unnamed prophet, whose alabaster jar
broke up a party,
recalls that Jesus told the guests:
"'By perfuming my body she is anticipating
its preparation for burial.'"
Such a fuss at the meal,
and how scared she was that night!

Joanna muses
what the palace would say
today.

Every body tells a story.
Does it matter who's who?
Who
is so wondrously
scared:
Talking oddly.
Seeing differently?

One settles back down
where the Cross-connection
with Resurrection
is unobstructed.

The dancer just wanted to prance on the Rock.
She laughed and she leaped
and didn't quite make it.
Not the first time;
not yet.

Someone sits on the ground,
and just doesn't get it.
She too is blessed. Still in place,
she will tell her own story . . .
and be believed.

It will be Precedent-Setting.

For church,
what is seen and heard
rising round The Rock
is the relevant Easter Experience.
In very human terms,
this is Easter from the Inside.

A woman perceives that the Dreams of Pentecost were spoken of all her daughters.

A Mother and Four Daughters

(Acts 21:8-9; Joel 3:1; 1 Cor 12:7; 14:1)

I don't know who you are
but you look like me,
and like people I know.

You are for real,
you who are so readily missed
or dismissed without a pause, in scripture.
Hardly legendary (even loosely),
your account is contained
in Nine Words,
three of which define you by your father.

"This man had four unmarried daughters gifted with prophecy."

You are having quite a time
in this Stolen Moment recovered.
I gather you.

101

In a space of your own,
made of paint messing around on pure new linen,
you assemble, you astonish.

You do have staying power.
The prophetic Message you send
is seeing the light:
God gave Light a human face.

Your inclusion seems Inspired,
almost accidental.
Incidental Prophecy,
intrusion by appointment
at this breaking hour of church.
Sisters of Wisdom,
friends of God and prophets,
the prophecy is *you*.

The Moment of Truth slips through
and hangs around,
looking familiar.

Behind the scenes and between Nine Words,
more than a glimpse Occurs
in a place called Caesarea.

Particular faces develop,
enveloped in Charism,
giving form and substance
and style
to a moment in time, of Acts
unrecorded,
overcast in red—radiant red!—
in light of The Flame.

In the house of Philip, deacon and evangelist,
whom The Spirit sometimes whisked away,
a happening of early church
is cast by women,
wondrously unscripted.

Their singular kind of sentence,
their storyline rarely repeated,
is tucked away in Acts
among details
of Paul's visit to the hometown of Philip:

"This man had four unmarried daughters gifted with prophecy."

It's meant to be
a salutary sentence about *him*,
within its period and without parentheses.

There
is a given mystique,
that opens to much
by saying too little.

Oh, this is not a Last Kind of word,
those Nine!
Scriptural women are left
dangling a Line
of free-standing Verse, unattached
and underdeveloped.

I like to presume that Their-Mother-His-Wife
—unmentioned—was also around the house somewhere.

The person who was always presence,
not absence,
comes forward with her handwork
signed,
quietly entering into
     a family experience
     of Word
     broken over bread
     that she made.

This is Entrée.

It is good to be free
to travel light
and to own up to Vision.

"I shall pour out my spirit on all humanity.
Your sons and daughters shall prophesy,"
church had been told
on its Day of Wind and Fire.
Beyond herself,
a woman perceives the Dreams of Pentecost
spoken of all her daughters
as collective Charism is manifest among them.

She is the visionary
in Joel's recurring words,
presenting Gifted Women
to Prophetic Church.

It was like her.
She would know.
Her eyes recognized
that Spirit glow.
This is Mystery in Plain Talk.

Clearly focused,
she exemplifies an original kind
of authentic gospel dreamer.
Fully awake.
She's been churched long enough
to be a little cheeky.

But not heady.
The undocumented mother of four daughters,
prophets represented in Nine Words of Acts,
is wise and old enough
to remember
much . . .
some of it relayed on her face and hand.

But then,
women, to be church,
had to develop a certain Good Crust.

She had learned about "belonging" . . .
everyday,
all the way from light to dark,
from inside and outside a door, or more,
and probably never was whisked away.

The partner who lived with risk
and whose hand raised up prophets
must have been a particularly prudent
and spiritually mature woman.
(These specific qualities were sought in The Seven,
including her husband, selected after Pentecost
to assist the apostles
and free them from table-work.)

When Paul on his travels
put his foot in Philip's door,
The Wife was right at home with The Daughters.

"Set your hearts on spiritual gifts—
above all, the gift of prophecy,"
Paul of Letters wrote to the churches,
ranking prophets second only to apostles
on his celebrated List.

"To each person the manifestation of the Spirit
is given for the common good," he taught.

There is nothing timid or tepid
or tentative
about any of four sisters
when The Spirit anoints.

Prophecy is light put to language,
and Light
is at the heart of
the art of Wisdom,
who Dances Around.

Sisters, four of a kind,
express facets of wisdom
from a fourfold perspective . . .

107

One, who speaks, is Truth Telling:
    light eyes her soul
    and heartens her lips.
A second's Involvement is Frankly with God,
    empowering the flowering
    of honest, earnest Prayer.
Another, Truly Listens . . . learning, discerning
    Truth with Compassion
    in humankinds of ways.
The fourth, in turn, Asks Questions,
    aware of the messes and stresses
    of getting to Real Ones.
The questioner does happen to look like
her mother . . .

———————————————

    One of the most prophetic poetic Peculiarities
    reflecting on women of church
    is a free-style of Verse
    that seems almost Irrelevant.
    It may go the distance.

We stumble in
where church is,
and mumble on
of prophets
with Scripts.

Vision falls behind
as far off, far out.
Too many stay
with beginnings too long.

Gloom and doom shroud and cloud
the proverbial Image of Prophet,
no longer confined to the world of religion.
The gospel Prophet, however, is marked
by the Folly of Hope.

Prophets and pilgrims assemble
at the moment Now
in church of all places
to get beyond
a Start,
without intentions or pretensions
(only tensions)
that *ours* will be a Last Word.
Astonishing!
How holy to be good
by not stifling ourselves!
Four of Our Kind are only beginners.

Fire pouring out of Oil and Water
will always bring out More of God,
largely Unscripted.

As you have noticed.

———————————

Notes on scraps of paper,
scribblings that didn't fit somewhere.
Most have to do with bread.

When the painting was planned,
bread was there—
off in a corner.
No table.
No overload suggested.

Just small, for fear of losing Focus.
Well, bread moved around
and came out a number of times.
It never went far.

"Bread is so basic
it is simply—and unobtrusively—there,
marking Christian community."

"*Any* Christological Moment
gets better with bread!"

Enough.
Sign it.
Keep it movable.

The Greatcoat of Many Colors is an old artist's smock, daily smudged by its Wearer. She's been working!

The Wisdom of Color

(Adapted from Wisdom 7:10-12)

The Greatcoat of Many Colors
is an old artist's smock,
daily smudged by its Wearer
in all colors of light.
She's been working!

Color *is* light, in more than theory.
This is practice. It was ever so.

Color explodes when it breaks into gray.
You, Spirit of Wisdom,
originated the image,
woman of color.

Hello again, my sister.

You made Hue
and Intensity and Value
in the first Creative Word:
Light!

113

Those dimensions of color
that every painter knows
have a New Application now.

Gestating directly under your heart,
Light is always in process of being borne.
Dropped?

    Way-Back-When
    you looked on a Void
    with Radiance
    that still neither blinks nor yawns.
    Gray appeared lifeless
    and Color was Prime.

    So much depends on the Source of light!
    God-one,
    whom we tend to restrain or retain
    in blacks and whites,
    you ordained Color
    so light could amplify, diversify,
    and get around.

    The Teaching Artist in you
    opens her hands and lets go—
    to develop People
    in creation skills.

Prophet of sisters,
who also loves brothers,
nudge us.
Budge us.
Smudge us.
Keep that brush of your hand
coming our way. Such a stroke!
Coat us!

Billow.
At high noon, gospel time (shining in the sun),
you throw up your hands.
With apparent abandon,
you toss Brush and Canvas.
In all the universe,
they gravitate toward a Speck.
Earth.

"*You* bring tomorrow!"
is your challenge to prophets,
often tired gray.
By nature, it seems,
most of them are women.

Don't you ever give up?
You were never born yesterday!

Threads of fabric stream through space
like a breakaway umbilical cord.
"Weave!" you say in the Wind.
"Don't let it unravel!"

We catch a glimpse of raw New Linen,
primed—not just salvage—
and still up for grabs.

It is the unfolding gospel Scroll,
meant to take us who take it
where we've never ever been.

An air of Gray has a way
of getting under the skin.
It locks people into a comfort zone—
an intermediate range
between black and white.
Colorless dull . . . but
gray can put up a front.
It often obscures you.

The Making of Church
is yet to be seen
as the Finest of Works.
Its colorant is the gospel
humanly experienced.

Throughout the world, the hue and cry
is *your* Outcry for justice
in light of the Color of Skin.

The Cry of the Poor among us
is *your* Prophetic Word.

This is the Value
you pursue with such Passion.

So many times, in so many ways,
when you hound us,
we run.

Bear down, dear Laborer.
Who will deliver you
of light?
Who can conceive of Being
in such an awe-ful plight?

Push us to pursue
your timeliest gifts.
To get what drifts!

"All these delighted me,
since Wisdom brings them,
though I did not then realize
that she was their Mother."

It can be prayerful to ponder
the face in the mirror.
Do women image
a less-likely God?

God of Many Names is pictured
brown, black, red, white, and yellow;
now the spectrum comes in *tones*
to be sure to be Inclusive.

We see Jesus in city streets,
mountain villages,
and more likely—still—
as a babe in a manger.

And you, Sophia, and El Shaddai;
bakerwoman, sweeper,
nursing mother, mother hen,
mother eagle. We have found you.

All that and more.
Complexions, reflections . . .
Color seems to swirl.
But God of New Creation,
you never were a girl!

———————————————

God of Would-Be-Artist-People,
come to the void!
Impress us
with your Variety of Expression.

Bring out new forms of Beauty
that are borne deep within.

Be for us
a holy sense of woman,
a unitive sense of self.

Complete the delivery!

Show up in space
we haven't yet seen
and can't even guess at.
Emancipate
what is already within us.

Bear with us,
Spirit of Wisdom.
Your light conveys.
Its full color is hidden
under the folds of
that Luminous,
Voluminous Coat.